The Rivers Are Inside Our Homes

The *Notre Dame Review* Book Prize

VICTORIA MARÍA CASTELLS

THE RIVERS
ARE INSIDE
OUR HOMES

University of Notre Dame Press
Notre Dame, Indiana

University of Notre Dame Press
Notre Dame, Indiana 46556
undpress.nd.edu

Published in the United States of America

Library of Congress Control Number: 2023937447

ISBN: 978-0-268-20566-9 (Hardback)
ISBN: 978-0-268-20567-6 (Paperback)
ISBN: 978-0-268-20568-3 (WebPDF)
ISBN: 978-0-268-20565-2 (Epub)

In memory of Emily Robinson Reeves,

my beloved, genius friend,

and Nico,

loud musical theater enthusiast and unforgettable writer.

You both were treasures to me.

CONTENTS

III

ACKNOWLEDGMENTS

Many thanks go to the following journals in which these poems originally appeared, often in earlier versions:

> *The Journal*: "Hurricane Advice from Your Sister," "To Make a Balsa Because You Have To"
> *Notre Dame Review*: "Cajas de Muerto," "Trilocation"
> *Quarter After Eight*: "On Both Sides, Water"
> *Reservoir*: "Go to the Smallest Room Right Now"
> *Stonecoast Review*: "February Fifteenth MDCCCXCVIII," "Necropolis"
> *Tinderbox Poetry Journal*: "Cuba, Boasted Rival of Swiss Chocolate"

Thanks so much to my parents, Ricardo and Diana, for their excellent advice and many wonderful meals, and to my sisters Carolina and Carmen, for their sense of humor and chisme. And of course, to my uncle Mario for his great stories and encouragement. I couldn't be a writer without you all!

Of course, thank you so much to Amy Fleury, for introducing me to poetry. I wrote my first real poem in your class, and it forever changed my life. Thank you also to Chris Lowe, Jacob Blevins, Rita Costello, Wendy Whelan-Stewart, Melanie Ritzenthaler (co-founder of World's Worst Book Club), Nayelly Barrios, Dorsey Craft, Cesca Waterfield, Luci Mirelles, and Eric Nguyen.

Thank you to Eduardo Corral, Gina Evers, Teya Schaffer, and Elizabeth Threadgill for your invaluable critiques at the Postgraduate Writers' Conference.

Thank you to Alfred de la Rosa, Christine de la Rosa, Valerie Barreiro, Ashley Murga, Venessa Vargas, Gussie Danches, and Crystal Garcia at Miami Arts Charter School. Thank you to my students past and present, including Serena Lozandi, Bryan Robleto, Maia Tasker, Tyler Vivas, Nour Abradabo, Kathleen Castro, Gabrielle Quintero, Naomi Wong, Maddy Barker, Lily Hernandez, Ximena Galaz, Maria Arango, Zach Tsokos, Angelina Gomez, Max Alvarado, Lily Barmoha, Bindi Loveland, Ella Richmond, and Isa Matthei. Having the opportunity to read your poetry has been an incredible gift.

Thank you to Alissa Del Riego and Norma Rodriguez for your friendship and wisdom, and also to Lili and Eduardo Del Riego and Daniel Cardenal.

Special thanks to my group chat, Leah Fisher, Jess Feinman, Aubrey Kay Turner, Lauren Haigler Henderson, and Anne Mauldin Osborne. Many thanks as well to my college roommate, Candace Daugherty, who read very early works of mine.

Thank you to Lillian Ros and Matilde Castells for the memories they have left and the courage they have shown me.

Finally, thank you to Orlando Ricardo Menes, for the brilliant analysis, intelligence, and support. This book would not be possible without you!

I

Trilocation

Planetary Communistic Infamy:
the Cuban young
flourishing the moon farms,
as if guavas were a common itch
and the stars themselves
could speak like
Leninists. NASA would be sent
manifestos.

A lunar backup plan, having taken
the Castros under an ensured
corpsedness and expelled under
galactic seal, this skin too misspent
to purify under chicken bones
and praying, ultra-zombi
remains in search of a malleable
galaxy where all of it could work again.
The rest pushing on through dust and
globe, the planetary rover now a
taxicab, el comunismo rooting the
stars and dreams of eating ice giants
like granizados bought
on the street.

Dejando atrás, a dream and memory,
the memory a dream and the dream
memorized to tell the Miami-like
children you have too now, further

hijos de exilio—to say to them,
no more of these Atlantic centuries,
that dirt-on-water overgrowth,
Caribbean seabed risen to air;
we are the moon as it runs out.
And for that other land we declaim against,
an asteroid pushed from terrestrial pit:
only deadly mental perfection,
the nostalgia of island on earth.

February Fifteenth MDCCCXCVIII

My hold on Cuba is
spiritualist, like the US Navy
on the battleship *Maine,*
bones buried and honored
in the Cementerio de Cristóbal Colón;
trying to learn what it means to be
Cuban and dead for one year;
before taken back, Arlington-
assimilated, American bound,
and forever to speak in Spanish
because they learned
how to be Cuban,
more Cuban than me:
dead in Havana for one year,
and I living for none.

But if I could ask if you still
know of the others, their cells
drifting across the bay in contrast
to your bones, comrades unclaimed,
disinterred, tunneled from
themselves in the Caribbean Sea,
to these others, say, you gave us our
freedom, it lasted fifty-six years—
You have doubled that in water.

If one could swim there
and feel them on the skin,
it would take all these years to forget it.

5

Necropolis

para mis abuelas

My love for you
is of the sarcophagi
of Havana;
sea-suppressant cases and corpses
buried inside the soil that still
tastes itself Communist. When run
down in seawater their cells
cannot wrinkle away, break back into
the ocean:
they are marble
and immune.

The seawater has
not found into us.
I think under your skin
broke the angst
of a beloved human angel,
as if in the Isle of Pines,
the dead under el descuido,

marked as a stained white stone
in its American citizen cemetery
covered under the marabú.

I think you died
and never came back
to where you wanted to go.

To Make a Balsa Because You Have To

Islands are hungry but never
dangerous. If the nation is a police
state and a body can summon only
knives into guts and fruits are the
objects in black market, not guns;
then maybe everyone should feel safe,
if not from a stomach or the blood
that seeps in you.

Though like Cuba, Venezuela
has balseros too now.

We know that paradise escapes paradise
and that rafts are never new things.
Talking of Caracas marriages under night
long replaced by marriages of lunchtime,
where safety shines brighter and forever
bonded to bodyguards. The world outside—
ransom, and inside—teatime. Blood flowing
inward. Darkness is either forest moved to air or
the sun not grilling faces, when trees cannot stop
their swallowing, and oceans are only burnt people
buried in water. And to know that new victims
eat flamingos too now like sharks eat Cubans,
the loss of limb and beak and life and weight,
since water is never innocent and if there
could be beaches everywhere: that water
would float you, instead of under, away.

Hurricane Advice from Your Sister

When you know the hurricane runs
near you hurry around with a treasured
bit of death knowledge, terror the zany
edge that is tasted under the weak roofs,
windows so wide as kingdoms,
the ceaseless prayer as if for loved ones,
please stay oh God oh, por Dios
stay stay always—be here for both of us,
but is our house the anti-storm
or the first body to flood
and your throat to turn to a garden hose
and must I swallow the cyclone so my
teeth may work as a crown
in this kingdom of water
and I can save you.

Guardian

Bewildered by cookbooks,
lately arrived in New Jersey,
no more Havana, no more kitchen help,
beachy mornings to send three children
off to sink in pools for much of the day.
Only there are new American treasures:
a tin cartridge of bobby pins, its hoard
of spider legs to hold up your hair, emptied
perfume bottles, liquid soap poured inside
like cleaned gold. The three sons with no
English, and that husband to worship, to feed
him and feed him, no microwave buttons
to touch his fingertips, your untalented
scholar hands attempting to put together
a sandwich from a husband's duties freed
of cold cuts and housework, all past money
incinerated and tucked away and put to memory.

Feeling alone.
Old British novels to be read and shared
in the cold Jersey air, deals and sales
and cheap things never-ever surrendered
to scrap. The fossilized mixers, tin cans gleaming
like royal crowns, emptied olive oil bottles
converted to Yankee riches; a pantry
of immigrant gold.

And yes there are Spanish textbooks to write,
earn Castells family money as if in secret,
but you have those meals to prepare,
carrot and guava and cow's tongue,
Matilde a cook's name for a hungry man
to cry out for—

Andrew

As a child my mother
fought against the door.
She tried to hold the sofa
against the buckling thing,
praying her weight to fatten
to gold as the door became a wing
reaching in, and in, and in,
a rippling shield changed
to a hinge of evil while a few yards away
the ceiling rippled, levitated
and fluttered back, and the tree fell,
the car crushed under it;
the radio apologized, its windows
cracking, anchors headed to the bunkers
and no more updates, it was time to run, run, run;
so under siege, the door squirmed
and my mother rocked against it.
My sisters cowered and I bid my body
to faint through the storm.
Waking up to my mother the conqueror,
our candlelit home,
dew-breached and breathing
in heat, a sister already sickened
from dirty water, our house cramped
with family, upright, survived,
and when asked of the struggle
at the gates of our home,
I remembered nothing.

Wishing Game

There were two women in the garden
and between them, ponds opened up
wide enough to hide both for a time.

They ran and ran far away as long
as they could, though paradise
was a map for runaway wives
and you'd soon end up back
again to the original point.
Swimming was the same.

They were moody, scrubbed harder
and weeping between hiding places;
as well as that the man pursued
them and sprang them out from
under hemlock and water.

I have been gifted with choice, he said,
the mother of all beings, to replace
the dirt that does not talk to me.

And he declared pure one hand
pulled out of pond, a leg and a
bit of face and length of hair,
and so she was chosen and thus birthed us,
humanity spilling out like angelic desire—

Trees ran and twisted from the earth. Fruit sprung like stars.

Afterwards,
the women sought out the seraphim
to join together their grouped wings
as shelter, rustle in silence underneath
the foaming sun, newly formed scales
to glisten under fountain and sweetness
of water, hiding their long necks with
their loosened hair.

Stars grew underneath us. Sickness and debt took all men away.

Nectar formed in our ponds and we were not yet bid to leave.
More babies grew from the ground though the feathers on their backs
were more like birds and they opened their beaks to be fed.
The snake held back a little longer. Sin gathered like sweat
and crusted like dew at the trees. Every day, the jungle grew,
soaking us. We drank from the jawbones of water serpents
and asked if we were not meant to stay.

Ask us if we did not warp and buckle, an oasis below Heaven,
to spring like cancer and rain the land in bad brew.
Let us know if we did not smile, all of us, when you asked
if we did not have more spoil to give, if we were not
overrun in bounty and flame, seasoned with composite
children, why we could not accept the exile offered us,
why we had charred to annihilation our own kings.

Migration

Havana and Miami,
double paradise.
To have and not have at all.

So how to explain, English and Spanish
roasted together as one, hot and pleasing,
our beaches under a distant portal, time
rupturing and hurricanes passing between
like forgotten family members, while buried
is the carcass of boats among us.

Until how long is it 50 more years or if the continents
could seize together, a collision of capitals; to exit
la Torre de la Libertad, which clothed my mother
in Miami, and find yourself small under el Cristo
de La Habana, grand Jesus on the hilltop, tremors
cleaning the bloody waters so the drowned ghosts
of our immigrant ocean could unwind their deaths
and talk to the living once more.

The Short Exile

To flee for so little distance,
as if to exchange your home for
a neighbor's house and spy on it
from a window. Garden wilting.
Party ongoing.

The road breaking down. A scent
of sea in the air.

Abuela Lillian spoke about
going home but didn't
really mean it.

CSS *Stonewall*
Stationed in Havana Harbor

The battleship arrived late,
namesake already dead.

A Parisian gift to honor Confederate
friendship with a European king,
and the French yearning for cotton,
always cotton, and one breaking
branch reaching out to a
dying government in Virginia.

Napoleon III, little nephew,
last monarch, hombre de sueños:
it could have been his eternal
Catholic empire run with the dreams
of the Mexican marquis and an archduke
sent to rule them. God and crown
and sparkling Earth.

The American South burned,
el Emperador de México killed,
a chapel built out from the
nephew's body in British exile,
and so forever we switch lands
and ways of speaking since home
is another word for escape.
We run, we hatch, we bury
our mothers across different places—

Today, Russian spy ship
Viktor Leonov arrives in the
Havana harbor. An American
cruise ship appears; witnessing
the other, they break apart like
broken flowers, sailing through
hot Caribbean waters on the
path to fantasy, this pearl
erupted from Earth, island
of dew and Communist tide.

On Both Sides, Water

In the Sierra Maestra mountains,
Castro and his men longed
to enter Havana. My family
waited to cheer and welcome
the men as angels. The key to
paradise was in this pilgrimage,
but who could be entrusted to
guard it? The gates of the capital
opened and the food from the
heavens disappeared. Evacuations
surged like a curse of God,
hallucinating for American shores.
Our exile arrived like a burning spring.

Che in Technicolor

One day he glimmered.
Famous black hair twined into colors
of Cuban flag under water, the ivory
and midnight and wild blood turned to
hues of more sparkling bonds,
there in the nighttime boardroom,
fatigue jacket repurposed
to radiant drama,

a blinking spectrum of
economic perplexity:
sugar price decline, cascades
of rationing, inability of medicine,
milk, belts, bras to be found.
My grandmothers bolted from
store to store.

La comida desapareciendo like the reversal
of bread, disappearance of fish,
rarity of cow. The prisoner camps
shone in lights. A gate of fire appeared.
They chose to burn. Dream after dream,
seven years of famine broken onto
eons of Cuban limbs.

The bruised moon flashed in agreement,
and revolutionary brothers died. The first
cabinet died. Allies died of disfavor. Che shines.
He always shines, cloak of glamor and diodes,
example leading into a new dawn,

stars for each killing.
Bullets will sprout on the seafloor,
lighting a dream-path
out from our long shortage.

Cuba, Boasted Rival
of Swiss Chocolate

It is good to own a good many things, at least soap.
To own the ice cream in your hand. To wash
your hands if there is money for it. To split
apart a cone in your hands if you hold
it too tight with feeling, and the wafer soaks
and you bite into it and there is ice
cream and what wafer is made up of.
Your teeth feel it all. You say to me
that it is time, you want to see the streets
your grandfathers now dead grew up in,
or la embajada maybe, the cemetery, and also
Coppelia, the heladería built after they were born,
fled (but before they died), to see the
ice cream there and to taste it—yes in the sixties
it was desired to have more ice cream flavors
than the United States, because that is important,
and important to try out: ice cream, milk,
sugar, whatever few flavors available, maybe
sugar cane, you who have never cut it
but you know others in Miami who had.
You drank sugar cane juice at supermarkets
growing up and taught yourself to like it.
Those cannons you desire to hear announcing
themselves in the Havana morning, not for
Cubans now, it's for visitors like you who go visit,
and for those ghosts of grandfathers now dead,

but I don't know if when they die they cross
the ocean or if they only tolerate
the feel of democracy and peninsulas.
If you want the exile to wither,
then it is good your grandparents do not own you,
the young can never be the same as the old in any case—
the ones who would forbid you,
you who have never seen the mystery,
or tasted anything at all, and all
for the grandfathers now dead whose ghosts
may be political, and you say you want
to taste the flavor of ice cream.
Are ghosts, or humans, more politically minded?
What do you care for when you die?
What are the flavors telling you?

Go to the Smallest Room Right Now

You can choke on the moon or in this hurricane,
weatherless haven or house rubble, the helpless
streams from the ceiling as adrenaline tries to whip
you up to a river powerless as the sea crashes down,
or the rocks. A yard exhausted with water. Eyes
sinking. Your skeleton tries to heave itself from
your body. It wants to cleave to the recesses
of your door. Your body fears to be the failed door.
Your hand made of crushable cement lingers on the
branches and the water is the dream that dents you.

Mothers' Warnings

Back when the land was Spanish plunder,
the great-aunts of my grandmother
encountered the horrid night.

They danced and joked at la fiesta,
caught up in madness and humid
celebration, the last ones, those doomed
maidens, tender-hearted chismosas,
crinoline creatures.

But as guests of the house they would not stay.
In our own beds, they said, in our own nightgowns,
like wraiths over our pillows to dream our
enchantment; we will never sleep miles
from our home.

They insisted as all women in my family often insist.

The journey was short—
la bahía de Santiago de Cuba
under dark and moon,
an engine's low monstrous call
to tired ears, and the gasoline
used itself up and the boat
lost its heart.

The sisters leapt into the ocean.
Silk skirts too heavy and like shuddering
dragonflies long-haired and dreaming,
las damas could not swim, beating
their arms like dancing sparks,
and boat and woman overturned.

As a child afraid to leave her house,
Abuela Lillian would tell my mother,
do not tarry, always leave a guest's home
on time, the price is ultimate.
Whatever you do—
never cross the sea too late.

II

Rupture, Alternating

I

The air grows hot and the building dies.
The building stops speaking the harsh
light that never bleeds warmth. Everything
becomes a glow. Relinquishment. Coolness
still in the larger hallways. Becoming
hotter. An alarm; faint, persistent, rushed
nothing-sound. No one speaks. It is dark
and light mixed together. The real lights
don't work. The sun tries to shine through.
You can see it through a window.

II

The building is a tower. You had light on your
hair and I climbed gold and sun split apart in my
hands and you had to brush off the rugs on my fingers
with a comb. And it was of your hair and I wanted
to braid strands on the floor and have you tend over
me, our gazes fixed until we fainted.

You marveled at how my eyes looked
beautiful to you.
They had the roundedness
of earth, hot lasers, a slope burning.

III

You found me maimed,
far from the tower,
garden of radish and rapunzel.
I carried the ruin on my head.

You made me cut
your hair, and your hands
followed me on the
scissors and your hands
wept at the blades.

Blood palmed my neck
like I had died,
cut hairs prickling my face
like new sideburns where
your blind touch
found me, your palm
beginning on my jaw,
fingers touching my ears
and you breathed
your cries into them.

IV

The mind can separate. The shadow is long
from its death. She has told you that this
is life. Still feeling the push of the ground
and through the window before
you met air, hapless bird, insufficient
prince, dark failure. We are a dead building.
Once she left her hand on your wrist
until giving it permission for it to
leave you. Standoffs, dreams of starving

inside a lake as small as a well and waiting,
wanting the other to drown. You had to
watch the water until it grew dead.
Your skin whitened from the water
until eyes did not work and you had to
find her hair and pull it like twine
to escape her.

Yes but always from the start
she left you wondering—

doesn't she,
didn't she?

V

You climbed the rope
of my hair and found it
beheaded from my body.
The witch threw you and you fell.

If there is water in the desert,
then we will find it.
If this is the desert,
then there is a chance
to find you in it.

VI

The long-ago spectacle of a deep fall,
and I try to brush it off and carry on without
eyes, and your hair grows longer and you fall
to your knees and you don't look at me.
The tower is a memory

left behind.
You say, I give up.

But I did try, you see, and you did not mean
to lose your hair, and your skin hurts,
your skin was hurt from the
sun. The desert will always toil.
Somewhere there is the ocean.
We are in the desert.

If I could hold you one
day on the beach.
Our bodies would be turned
out by tide
and the sea would
run with it.

VII

In the beginning,
bound together
like knots, we curled
into each other.

I caught the pain in my head
when you climbed, and you
saying sorry, hands careful on my
hair, but she caught me unwinding:
braids torn away from the long tower
and you fell down from it;
you said you screamed
my name once and the name
of the king, your father.

Thorns met you at your eyes.
I waited motherless for you.

Time extended like the fall
of my hair.

VIII

The tears meant for me
were turned into a reservoir
to feed yourself.
The tears were made of sun.

We know that the water is fading
and ocean not with us.
We know, we know the water fading.
The ocean is far
and we know.

For her to say:
this is what I feel,
this is what I taste,
and this is what
I think.

IX

It is only lightly burning
in the exile of the desert. We know
the remaining water is falling;

our knees are dry and
free from what little is left.
We cannot heal ourselves.

Are we a fever, he asks. I have
already lost you a thousand
times, and each time
it felt definitive.

I have felt the same.
We know that the water is spinning.
We lost your eyes in it,
we know that the lost blond rings from your
head are being pressed onto earth.
The eyes springing.

X

When the blades staggered inside
my hands, hair and blood mixed
to freedom, you tried to save its
motion with your tears but still you
failed and already they were punctured
and shaking from the wish to know,
and no magic left over for my eyes.
Our love is fullness and horror—
a tree growing underneath.

I already knew of my mistake,
to feel as you do
without the completion of your head.

XI

You turn to me and your
eyes are missing.

I say, sorry, the hair is in
your eyes still,
let me trace the hair
from your eyes. You left energy
somewhere on my head where
your blood roped into
mine. You touch the marks
of my scalp where my mother
betrayed me and placed
me in desert. My head
is a torn monument. My mind
bows beneath it.

We know our knees are down to the water.
And you tell me,
I still have some eyes
left, I do.
Let me feel it.
Let me make you feel it.
Just find it for me.
Just find it.

I take your hand and guide it
to water so you can
feel the bitter drops spinning.
You can feel the desert on your hand.
Holding it out like I could clean it.

Wanting to bathe your hand together.
Wanting to cup me so I could be water
rising in your hand.

XII

Or for her to say:
My mind,
I am lost in it.
You are the body.
You want to be lost in mine.

I want to put my mind
in your body
and see.

Las Princesas Bailarinas

The problem is that we should have stayed at the party forever.
That we went home when we shouldn't have, when there was
more party to be had. Dancing princesses under trapdoor and grove
and glittering tree, feasting on arrepas, ropa vieja, and deciding
that all good things had to remain secret. Beheaded and chopped,
our father cried over the scraps of our suitors, kings' sons squabbling
for kingship. We had pushed those sons to sleep; under herb and lust
they missed the party. So how innocent did they expect us to be—
steamed under passion, bewildered onto earth? Spanish-speaking princes
who taught us better curse words and spoke of islands to take us
deep inside the ocean, escape from fairy tale. We would rather die
than be caught and sent away. Yet they married us off and we lived.

Spicy, greased pits begotten to miracles and hot horror; thrusting life
outside of us. We became mothers. We would never go back. We
would never go back. Married off, oldest to youngest, eldest spinster
to weeping girl, and there was no more festejada, ni un pastelito, not one,
and our new husbands knew not of exile. Still screaming about islands,
los príncipes perdidos, jodidos, but we forgot Spanish anyhow,
and the party was done with, and we never went back.

María Antonia

My bisabuela passed,
and had to go underneath
for the death journey,
wrap herself in Cuban soil
forever, but refused,
and I mean *refused*,
to be buried with my bisabuelo,
long-eared progenitor and
ancestor of my long lobes.
She hated his cousin.

The shivery thoughts of such a soul
wandering the Olivella family plot,
inferior ghosts, delirious vapor
of disliked cuñados,
thus long abandoned to what I
will never see either,
the Class of 1923 School of
Medicine graveyard where
María Antonia lies instead, more
Communist-tainted mystery—
And yes, my great-grandmother
refused to give birth in so small a
zone as Zaza del Medio,
and so nine months flowered with
Abuela Matilde, María Antonia
herself a licensed obstetrician,

riding to Santiago de Cuba
without the company of a husband
to find more elegant air
and the birthplace she wanted.

Mujeres cubanas are the kind
to hate cousins and love
strange graveyards and
is it any wonder I burn badly
under orders:
for Cuban women,
their opinions mean so much.

Homemaking

The children draw the body
to sleep on the ground.
Staircases grow from stone
to shade the figure in slumber.
We love you, they say, if you wake.

The doors were born closed
and wait to house family.
Folded in light, a spring of iron
garlands a stairway,
dirty and neglected,
steps like dark teeth.
The form is flat and the stairs
are tilted. They draw their gods.
We can almost see it, they say,
the creature behind us,
eyes white and round, waiting to rise,
bread making of the body.
The dead move from floor
to floor.

Light bakes from one open
door. Bars and plaques
and chalk and crouching.

The children ponder and plan.
The body sleeps.
They wait for the hands to grow skin
and pull back their hair,
as long as a tower;
the fallen awakened,
for the three to grow four.
A recipe and a baptism
to hide what has been lost to us.

She shall be my wife, one says, when I am older.
She will grow and sprout into a bride, says another.
The last boy: she will love me forever,
she will ache me down and rattle in my throat,
our dark homes will turn into gardens.

The boys bow their heads.

Yes, the body says out from the floor,
there was murder here.

Tintagel

She remembers Tintagel—
plums without skin, seeds uncentered,
and how she ate them with gusto, magic
eating the fruits of the black trees
until the roots died and the knights
fainted, dreaming of another joust.

The rules split open, other-origined
witchcraft played out in battered lands;
visited by a stray hurricane, pieces of ocean
appearing one day through the shrubbery,
soaking through the twigs and the worms;
parts of seagulls materializing, banana skins,
then mangos, non-British foods falling
on royal heads, plantains sieved
with angry fingers, jabbing inside fruit,
finding pearl black rot, eating what she could:
strange gifts of a tropical cold.

One day a snake's head rose
from the earth, and another dozen
fanged crops, and they hissed at her;
Morgause cried out in hunger and premonition,
dreading the visits of Merlin, no friend to her,
bearded and ugly and lovesick, telling her
she had no power to change what was to come.

Her youth, the Tintagel gardens before
expelled to Camelot, twinkling and
sparse plums, exposed flesh, crazed flowers,
coconuts cracking on the grounds and vomiting
up the sea after too many spells.
The training ground for conquest, beaming
and black-frocked, agonized in foresight
and smiling, the future a terse knot in her head;
desiring foreign husbands and estrangement,
half-drunk from wine since she was nine years old,
acquiescing open mouthed lords at adolescence,
wrapped in prophecy, a lust that ran on forever.
She sought protection in mist and men,
a pale procedure, and Merlin did not help her,
stupefied and lost, tangled in dreams—

She didn't want to become a mother.
Grape-spent, she felt the skin
and pit of eyes on her.
And finally, the reunion.
She bowed low and said she had forever
wanted a family, a sibling.
The cloud visited her bed.
Her womb unfurled.

Caretaker

Yes, he asked you for a sandwich.
It was 1992, Hurricane Andrew already flooding
your basement and tearing apart your orange trees,
the two of you hiding out the category 5 in a closet.
And yes, you did it. It was 2 a.m. but you took
your flashlight to the powerless kitchen
and made him a roast beef sandwich.
You even put on mayonnaise.
The refrigerator was dead silence
and medium warmth, but you had not the heart
to throw away the food for him, despite the rotting
the future would bring, the maniac scents
you knew would tide out and drench.
There is no need to explain.
In case he might need nourishment, in case
your husband might call out your name.
You are beckoned and summoned and loved.

Matilde, Matilde,
the hurricane says to you
from outside the windows
besieged and surrendering,
from the garden leaning
and whipped, in pain,
a shedding of fruit and citrus.

Estoy aquí, estoy aquí,
you almost say in turn,
the roast beef offering
in front of you.
You knew his hands
were useless without golf clubs,
without air, without bread to hold,
small tasks to complete,
to order others and to proclaim.

You knew this was a trial,
bad story, the world that demanded
everything from you, another complaint to
seed and grow inside your skin.
Pain and sons and meal preparation
and exile. You would greet
the hurricane later. You knew.
You knew.

A Liking, Somewhat

At night I took what was given.
Pricked and plucked, little point
bristling, I bounced under storm
and I burned.

It was something to do.

My limbs weighed little.
My fingers shrunk like hot
flowers; in secret and under cloak,
I ate oats like a goat, quick and nimbly,
maiming and mewing—he didn't like
me eating at mealtime, a husband
to carefully wrap fingers over mine
and repeat, *para, por el amor de Dios.*
There was tenderness there. Under ceiling,
over bed, pillowed, rocking, I sensed
from under his fingers it did not matter
what I was, soft eyes and jellied neck,
so I was plum, curdled, caught, I squeezed
and melted from the top of my hair;
my ankles squirmed, in a moment of affection
dije que nunca podría vivir sin él,
and my husband said his beard turned
blue the moment he saw the ocean.

The bluish butter of his legs, bruised pox
under blue hair, chest ringing under
my fingers; a spreading love, gushing
eye of squid and nipple under midnight
until I too was lost in blue seed.

My husband, mi cariño, cariño, I chanted,
young and bored, dreaming—
I lived for something dark.

My hands never caught the blue.
Wanting as I did to enter his bones,
know the body better, why he burned
through the blue and hurt me and I had
nothing else to dream about,
one chamber unpardonable to us.

Was not the forbidden where we were meant to go?

Hate, boredom, affection,
it struck me blue and deep.
And what I found far from family
and home, long-haired women:
wives as lonely as I was.

A liking, somewhat, I told them.
A restorative, lightly treasured.
Both of us to live unburied,
desperate for night, sunk
in strange inclination.
He has never killed me—
he might never.

The man who does not love me more
than predecessors demi-haired
and dirty gowned, not long dead,
the rotten brides in the corner,
neck paused of breath,
breasts crushed of life.

I took what was spared
and could not live without it.
To choose a husband incorrectly
and to burn apart in bad dream.

We argued until sunset—*will you
not bury me, was I somewhat special*—
and my husband wept when he
strung me up by the ankles
and my hands dived towards
the floor—*de qué me condenes*—
for enjoying the sparse meals,
the pocked body, a friend,
I took what had been offered to me,
esposo azul and bored wonder;
we never choose right, I tried
hard to be happy, I gnashed through
it all, the blue disappearing.
Nights of mistake.
Now I can find no better, the one
husband, el único, el sagrado.

On a Husband's Next Family

There is a trick to divorce,
Lillian finds out.
Let the second wife in.

Let her pre-ordered, early son arrive,
then go and do not return,
rid yourself of island and spouse.

Let him multiply.
You are the scorching American secret,
chaste bulb, deposed ruler,
mystery unknown to future sons.
Accept the separation and let
the prince never find you.
Stay out in the desert forever.

Once a family, then a fruit growing
two skins, a ripened shelf breaking
and leading to trap door, grotesque
membrane bungled and boiled.
Rip his face from your wedding photo,
beheaded body in a suit,
executioner of memory,
ravager of unfaithful skulls.

Think on how beautiful you looked,
when you were happy, gleaming in
the white wedding gown, the sea so close
for so long, you never thought you could
be uprooted from the shore. Torn wife
expelled out into sunlight, exposed sand crab,
dazed sea bird, remade and running back
into paradise and sea snake and curse,
though never the right home
and the right story—
the gates have pushed us out.

Hot Season

I remember my aunt sweeping the fish
out of her house with a broom. These hours
belong to us now, they are gripped tightly to our
hands, however much caged fingers try to be freed,
this will batter and worsen, the wind will slap the trees,
topple the gardens, burst the fruit, scare the dogs
to wildness, storm-making in the ascent of midnight—

Our walls fall like lace.

Emergency

Yes, we are puncturable, we are bad drum,
I am a death call trying to escape
myself like a bird, yet I have never felt
so rooted. I am the bad tree easily skinned
and my skin could cover the world.

And the water is at the door.

Our clouds are burdened,
the air too big for us.
We hide like secrets
in our wet homes,
we swell as if sick.
Nodes bloom to thick
pearls, tongue to bulging
blue garden, gifted
and stuffed with
the sea. We meet
our roofs like Heaven.

Please know that amidst
our flooded brains,
in the hands that break
off and reach for you,
we will think of you with us
until the waters end and
the wilderness is remade
once more.

If the Water Is Hot
and Does Not Warm You

We multiplied like spores in the heavens.
Eyes clotted with waterlily, we blossomed like ghosts
at the creek, protozoan maidens without shield,
strength, or warrior's luck, hair glittering
like onyx bitten to black streams by the gods.
The starriest part of our eyes focused through
nightfall against our challenges; stone throwing,
diving down the longest, holding breath without
crying out. Everyone spoke of our loveliness.

Budding frogs jumped from our hands.
Like everyone else, we attempted joy.

Sometimes our screams would quit at
the brook, seasons of lust and capture
and shining nymph, half-immortal son
after son getting curious and hearing
of choice bounty. A lineage of plunder.
And cousins doing spellwork and creating
little pig-men out of sailors, eating
the island pork secretly, or humming
disasters down to ships, lyric bound
and breaking, harpies showing off
their bird legs in the sky, mountain sisters
assembling the carcasses of Diana's hunt;
we only felt polish and envy.

Meanwhile, the fauns never left off their chase
of us, hopeless ankles and flowered braids in flight,
running through hill and meadow, fur and claw
in the wreckage of our stumbling.
Bruises under our wrenched hair, blemished
patterns of split skin like we could die damned
in their trembling arms while they kissed us,
blood like passion boiling through the wells.
Hands to rip at our arms to hold us down,
ecstasy on the lakefront, goats who gripped
our tongues as if to swallow in angel spit,
cleanse their loins, to pucker at the ones
who did not reach the water and collapsed
mid-makeout, sullied pure on the grass,
dreaming of monsterhood.

They made us wives, or not, and thrust
crowns of windflower on our heads.
They dared us to smile at them and say no.
Like angry squids, skeleton of shell
and blood of runny ink, we terrified
ourselves throughout the bone-breaking.
And gods could not resist the parties followed
by weddings, limbs for seeking in and crawling
out and replacing each other. We shimmered
faintly and cried out in the groves. Crushed
under their hands, we prayed for deformation,
tentacles reassembled from our hair, bull
horns on our back, holy prayers answered,
titan palms, our wrath mountaining
without end under gem and feast.

Maiden without Hands in the Exile

What putrefaction I would choose to layer
and wrap tightly until it smoked my blood.
Desperation unaided at mirror. For what is
the largest planet made in another, love unbirthed
in you, and already my hands were nulled where my
father axed me and sacrificed me to our other gods.
I did not want to be buried down to where Heaven
hides, transaction of daughter for finery,
since my father held his head and looked at the
sun while my heart burned up inside spots
and I saw the devil outside of me
and could only pray to God.

I could not remain. I made food
of the fruit in the garden.
The angel watched me.
I slept between the lawn,
sculptures, kingly trees; eyes stamped
with castle walls, stumps tied
behind my back.
You found me taking the fruit
with my mouth,
made my metal hands to put
on your body and pull.
I sat in a sewing circle as queen
and nodded at my subjects,
handing out silk panels.

What caused you to need
me spilled out onto grave?
To have this spoken.
Most days I'd marry you infinite times,
feet magnetized to church floor. Mountains
have formed on my back. I bear
down to the ground in the
dreams too sweet; how they dig
themselves down,
they stun themselves over mouth.
I am sharp-tongued, I say little, I sit afraid.
I have to follow my son from room
to room. I am tired. I want him to sleep.
Everybody dies in my dreams.
I need the sun of open day
and
I am tired.

But if I could ask
what is your heart racing against—
what battle does your mind beat to,
what does it mean not to care—what is
the quality of who I was that wound
through you and I left you like water.

I find myself in the story of another,
I've veered into terror, I went
from the miller to you.
The visit here is long, my life is marked.

If this can be discovered,
why does not everyone
take themselves to the fire?
I want to be baked into this earth,
I want to come out as apple pie.

I try to smile at my child. Squeeze
purpose to the expression.
Show off airs of loved
happiness as when I was queen.

How could I have known
that your rib cage was crouching,
ore sprouting, eaten over,
where that brittle jungle grows
while your heart steamed
as king. You turn my bones cold.
I grew strength like a garden,
night is where I greet my
ghastly feelings, I shrink and shrink,
piety forms plaster, though we'd made
paste by pure pleasure, hour,
hour, hour, hour that pile inside
but strength is a death wish
ignored and fortified
and inferior to happiness.

The silver was not for picking up spoons,
the silver was for touching him.

But I can't accuse you, you hold seas,
the explanation is vast, only bitterest water,
endless mistake, safe house inside forest.
I have heard the pacing outside the
chalked circle, avoided the devil's eyes
but it's you that makes me feel
holes in my hair. The instinct for sin
was never in me. Minutes break,
you've done too much, the rivers
have died, the angels have barbs
on them. Every day I droop,
stunned, when I reach for his robes.

You will hold new infants. I am not a
memory. The day passes. If you could
swallow the silver and understand.
I would hold up my arms, sleeves circling
air. Your face peering into the abscess.
Your fingers reaching like weeds
to the darkness of my dress,
I can feel them cling,
while I wonder
Why did grace penetrate?
Why did I feel so much?

III

Key to the Indies

Disturb us, Lord, when we are too well pleased with ourselves, when
our dreams have come true
because we have dreamed too little, when we arrived safely because
we sailed too close to the shore . . .
—Sir Francis Drake

Sea battles are our chronic pain, so let the bone break faster
under the pull of long glory and luster of cannon, to die
for water burial amidst the gold and the heavens by a choir
of foul-breathed mermaids. How my stockings have trembled
with want from the tall cloud of the crow's nest. The New World
a gift to tuck away under Queen and island, to her best battler,
El Draque, El Dragón, supreme sea heart, he who craves the salty
wind, singing psalms around a musket.

I do love God, for dominion and glory make my heart ripen
to a bomb of salt in nautical paradise. As of yet we have lost
the chain of Empire, to eat up Santo Domingo and Cartagena
though to leave behind San Juan and Havana like a battered
Hispanic dream. I conquer through my sleep and my head is a pearl
to die stuffed and stained in Panama, backlit British knight and hero
cursing for more wealth, the slaves mine, the sapphires mine,
the field and the sugar and the everything. The Caribbean is an agony
left behind, a trashing and exodus, dirt and dream and horrible desire,
and forever have I wanted island's earth so badly.

Oh I too will reach Havana again.

Camelot

The sword easy enough to
　　take from the summit,
king stamped and mystical.
Spindly, underfed, desperate boy
　　grabbling in rock,
dirt on young teeth, over hands,
clutching at the glint of a hilt,
　　water-driven, new lands revealed
　　through tourney and capture,

the many plated crowns,
　　lion heads in gold and
　　　round plumed stones,
an Ichthys multiplied
　　and flashing—
Helpers de-graving objects
from the ground, gifted to Arthur
for subduing city after city,
blood conquered and drank:
　　　　a naked
　　　　　threshing
　　　　in tribute.

Morgause
done up for him,
　　pink satiny fingers itching
　　　to open;
blood boiling from the ears.
　　　Her cries wrenched him

and Arthur asked her why she
   was so evil, witch so beloved,
   left him burning sore, weak in the
   heart
and brain, knees exhausted,
   and tongue scraped from all
         the damp ribbons of the body,
            bespelled and burning,

and kingly.

The battles never ended;
war beat against his mind
for he knew how flesh
could be blooded between and without,
glazed under visor and breastplate,
hands of empty.
      Skin of the sister he could strangle.
He wanted to apologize
but could not.
He was tired and wanted
what he wanted.

Cajas de Muerto

To scrub this land of communism well:
Pretty-syllabled Habana, cramped
hive, sewage gripped under bug
stewardship, to live without,
without much, and forever—
a car you did not need and
you did not need or have—
auto inheritance missed out on,
(you miss its memory), any engine
heirloom of the mind, to add
power to raft, one last
moving prayer to be
heard by coast and water.

Still grouped and clogged within
the white taxi roaming, walking
and roasting to the seaside, a few
windowed nights hearing the baby and
its noise, a mother and the clogged milk
—you cannot buy what is not
spilled from the body—the tourists
looking on lovingly, and what
of your cousins paid to know
the feelings of American
dollars rolled inside to fullness,
of yuma shows and phone calls
freed and split from satellites,

furtive gray stars in the balcony, agents of
Cuban interplanetary communication,
and if you too could follow the
pulse in the air to Miami—

Yet one more free family funeral,
eternal gifts of the government,
though the effort of them,
pushing up the coffin wood breaking
from the car, up the steps, up,
and who could wonder at the struggle of the body
to the chapel, but if your uncle could
have been more refrigerated, then
not this blood, oceanic insides
forming a sea for the corpse, raft
breaking, you holding it, shoulder touching
the blood and there is prayer for everyone.
To carry hot floods on your burns
wherever you may go. So we can burn apart
in the sun, a sea set aflame.

Superpowered

There are no powers adrift from dictators.
Nicolás Maduro can enter in you like chemo:
king of medicine, lord of cancer, ruler
of hospital beds. A royal hand enflamed
in kilowatts, a golden cloud of electricity
or brittle oil buried in a thunderbolt,
a Zeus and a czar.

Under the disappeared water, hospitals
are flickering kingdoms of mattresses
and prayer. You can feast and heal
in their blackouts, break apart air
in your hands and dream of light,
generators failing around you in stunned
voltage as darkness replaces oxygen.

But wait for the Cuban doctors arriving yet
at your door with votes and pills in hand,
a reelection for blood pressure medication
and fealty, a godly bargain. Wait for the spirits
of the dead to fill up the heavens, the assassinated
to wait for their turn and the autopsies to never come.
Let the police shoot in the throat who would
take to the streets. Protests dispersed.
Wrap the head under a plastic bag
and beg the body to breathe.

Maduro receiving the Sputnik vaccine:
he feels fine, he says. All is well.
The prisons are safe. He feels healed.

A Ruler Is Poseidon

Inside every man is a little capitalist treasure.
A stupid heart like a secret prize, algo pequeño
y desagrado, in rock hard dirt. A grave of coin,
an Eden of money—a resort paid for in power—
for each person wants a yacht, even without wages
to buy one, even were it submerged, if you had to
swim to the bathroom and the tub was a lake,
the refrigerator a pond, the hot tub some flooding.
A boat to hold on to the end of the world.

I have the superyacht. Hombre fuerte, macho,
I hold the trident as master of the sea, speechmaker
of dreams. I possess the communist fingers to
hold my gold close and charge and boil
the waves, baking the bread to fire until
the throats of my people close and they eat
my name. Castro, bitter rose, a bit of bread.

State radio will speak of my mythmaking,
small boat and fishing hut, the bass to stain
my fingers, multiply my hurts. Una soledad quieta,
for I am also the god of storytelling, avenging
soldier nunca muerto, todo corazón, crusher
of men, elected from the will of my people,
happy all of them.

One who knows when you find your private island,
go to el Cayo Piedra, sail on the Aquarama,
yacht gliding from engines gifted by Brezhnev.
Cubans may anoint rafts with engines excavated
from trucks and all Cuban cars are American.

Yet a Soviet engine will always make a communist dream.

Hide the island. The yacht. Dolphinarium. Chalet.
Escóndolo todo, single cow for each son, favored milk,
feast of dairy and crown, sea deity. Even if dead,
even if underneath the ground ahora mismo,
presidential beard fallen off and thinking of Cuban jail
and more teenage protestors to put in them.

Nunca muerto, not truly. Still I am the divine
seafarer desiring power, screaming horse
pushing back the waves and bountiful flood,
el comandante escaping the river of dead by yacht,
this mastodon boat amidst the Marxist fathoms,
a never-dying heart. Uncloned, unsaved, unclenched
jaw under the dirt—carve me out like a sea god,
change me to barracuda, lead me out to swim.

The Pirate

Queen Elizabeth circles near.
Every day the bishop of San Juan
leads wartime prayer under the heat
of God and men will catch fire
by the sea. The moon burns
above cannonfire.

The people of the island are already brought pustules
and fallen fingernails, grapes and horses, fevers,
sobbing pigs; invaders who have twisted
out from the beach and the woods,
European crusts quaking closer.

Yet the British will glow under the night.
Under lust and treasure, blazing timber,
Spanish prayer, the harbor is cleared,
Francis Drake chased out to Panamanian
shame, legend spooked and swallowed.
Island gold free to glimmer in La Fortaleza,
fortress by the bay; the Taíno withering,
the city soon to melt by Dutch fire.
Forests topple, dominion swells—

La Fortaleza, as for six hundred years the Governor's palace,
a place for portorriqueños to protest march after the death
of electricity and the long, powerless stench of hurricane.

The tide has gone too far. Oceans spin bigger.

Floridian cities have opened up like Spanish-speaking
blossoms to accompany the ghosts of forts and pox,
battles fought on land already lost and bloodied,
our storm-seasons growing like fury.

How Can You Make a Communist Flower?

To make a flower out of pseudo ham,
buds assembled, petals beamed out
to symmetry.

A Soviet harmony of equaled
roots deep grown, an invasive song long-
burning,

plant prefabricated and mild,
half ham-scented, overboiled under
Cuban sun.

Learning to swim then droop,
find extinction in the water,
risen from soil to make the sea,

to bleed your seeds to eat,
to sing and burn and stop
and try to burn the trees,

to leave Havana disassembled,
durable termite under flower,
folding seafront under light.

Diagnosis in Exile

A worm to be burned at the thought's center,
treatment to make your death more broken.
Ruined pancreas, the tumors surgeons cannot
break through as if the tide and the salt must
bear them back; too rounded, horned,
flora seeded deep, sprayed under the scum
of a husk, and making the skin itch,
pain to radiate under your house dress,
on the sofa quietly holding your knees
to your chest at Christmastime,
still reading books by Jane Austen
to find comfort in her.

The land is still banished, dreams
of reunion split in half and swallowed
under radiation. Exile reaching its expiration.
You have not outlived what bore you out,
the body's badly sprouted seeds to collapse
under the moon and explode in the organs,
wither by the sea, of homeland, patria vencida,
sirena desintegrando, bad song still luring.
It is never truly possible to die at home.
You will keep on remembering, out loud,
forever; the sea will flush out with the waste.

And yet we will never separate
a la distancia de la maldición acuática,
flood the mind in Spanish until
the beginning can be found once again.
Together we will cross over
what the water brings.

Metamorphism

They were promised kindness. We took our mates
to the forest and put them to the fire. Some will weep
and wave, eyes of oak and insect, rejecting our displeasures
and crying like captured flies. They had always felt so safe
in the woods. They warned us that our long braids would catch
on branches, our hair would break, armor didn't fit on us,
so scratched we would have to become. Beasts to shove
their noses against our calves and follow us from stream
to stream. We were to pet pigs under our palms, praying
for safety. And what grew from our heads was nearly
gossamer: gunked, spidery film, misshapen web leaking
spilled meals, enlarging our tongues and we were already
changed. If a god chased us, they had warned, bow down
and wait for their arms. Let the crystals in your pupils glow
even brighter and breathe in the bright cloud and let them
crave you until it is over. Collect the violets and go elsewhere.
Never turn woodland and dream of it; no good hands to smooth
down our fur and goat hide and extra bones. But dare us
to crush entire hands in our mouths. Lap at the herbs on the
tongue, hands on hair and clutching at our fetlock, dig at us
under the dirt. There was never enough to go around.
Guilt was never good enough to treat us well. The horse
and lust, echo and purge, our cantering jog, to spring over
the declining earth, clutch the horns on our heads and
finger them like fiddles. Burn them further. If they knew
snouts could save us, hooves to hurt those who hunt at
our ankles and chase us through every conceivable place,
every house and train and street and store. Yelled at by

a stranger in a sandwich shop and no one said anything.
March inside trees until the hollows spike with heat,
knock down the bark and nick our hands and break
our flutes. Drink up the soot and mist. Waking up
to play music. We are the unsafe; the air explodes.
Swallowing madness like fire. Though quiet with fright
in front of a tormentor, they note this and call him
comrade. Sharing a drink is an exchange of blood;
a man needs his tribe—worse it would be to be rude.
Swollen in bonfire, our protectors will crack with the
bearded trees, wingless and accepting, friends to many,
eating the spoilage as a last meal and promising
us all to never understand.

And for the Head, a Crown

Dictators are blossoms, or tiny little robes
to put on countries and hide the bodies within
and form a flower bed, necks wrapped in
tropical orchids, and over that the Emperor's cloak,
from which Marxist dew hangs like a promise of
moonlight over petals peeling from human skin,
robes yet writhing through limbs making roots
in the mud. Everyone knows the need for
a costume. Brings on the boots and the fatigues
and the earth.

Antilles Formation

Triple bursting volcanos: defeated,
spewing pods among the orange,
squelching fields. Steam drinkable
from the summit. Beaten, rolled,
gasped into by the early moon burning.
A record of lava shifted to mutant
lake changed to verdant monsters
of wood as our trees swelled to the
Heavens and with them brought rain.
Sputtering, breathless, floods
burst to green and reptiles
turned giant, spearing into the soil
all to wade in this water.
The kingship of floods;
the Terrible brought low—

Splitting rock, defeat of glacier,
eroded betweenness of Americas
North and South.

Tectonic blocks thrust
with a dream of uplifted arc
out from oceanic dust,
to form small sea countries
upon the early waters.

Thick fantasy clotted over
cold ocean, magmatic scars.

And the blood of the conquerors
would deface themselves onto me—
burned from inception,
I could find no water cold enough.

Run under, the Spaniards cried
upon me and thought of God
and wished to dig in deeper,
carve me of gold and sugar,
drink me to immortal frame.

Above, they incinerated what once was.
And they would call my body home.

The Rivers Are Inside Our Home

So that they may
ease their sickness,
the clouds find
antidote in our bodies.
In the drenched parts
we must wait, the rubble
of my family
upturned under plague.

So who will meet me
at the passing of the tempest—
who holds the key to disband us?

We are at the brink of house,
gripping the final door,
our hull's cursed last stand—

Shelter in Place

We gelled our hands to the cleanest of castles.
Absent of dirt, they protected us as best they could.
Deprived of touch, every single stone fell away
and we walked in loops of home
and mealtime, clean little lordlings,
chanting against the contagion
while the waters rose higher and
the rain gathered with the sickness
and we heard the sounds of beasts
walking on our roofs.

Havana Syndrome

Your brain becomes an alarm,
grasped and rung and turned over.
The sea fills up your stomach
and the rivers drain your heart.
They can't remove the ship floors
out from under you.
Nights are unrewarded with sleep—

though you carry on, another strange Cuban dream
of American extraction. *Sonic attacks*, offers one.
Hysteria, embassies alight with it, says another.
Concussions pushed out from earth.
A seething dream. The stars.

There could be explanations.
Diplomats who, one day, achieved psychosis.
Too much Spanish and heat, rare sea food
turned paradisical, monstrous and cosmic,
creating a supreme, stumbling race out of men.
Or you have heard of the crocodiles unmooring
themselves of the ocean and upending their mouths
at the shoreline, the Cuban Godzilla, how they dizzy
the stone by the sun-tired bay. Lizardy giants
to eat the food and break all soap; polish their skin
with dearly bought detergent, gleaming in dollars
and foreign bank accounts: these shining marauders,
they could never be cleaner or clean enough;
illness brought back, hide thick like rubble

and some myth is responsible and it is them,
a mutation at the water dreaming of the capital,
roaring with each footfall.

At night they take more chunks out of Havana,
and vomit the bugs at the sewers.
Eat at the stone and the quarry
and the food line.
It is said when they scream, embassies tumble
into Heaven and then back out of it, for paradise
is a kingdom that eats pain
and it can never be made enough.

The head is pierced, eternally.
The creatures are American or Communist
or foreign or they never left or were eradicated early;
they brushed by Spanish ships, they swallowed the larvae
and the Caribbean Sea still glows with infection.
If it were to glimmer in Miami,
it might open the earth.

Even the shadows of the ambassadors
are dizzy. They murmur and blur
when trying to match the body. Bells split
from their hands. *There is new sickness here*,
they say. *How easily the ribbons*
that tie you could come apart.
Witness our body unscrolling.

Fiery light at the embassy.
Sanctions screw themselves into the land,
the American opening ending, for the crocodiles,
for the sleepless, dreaming brains, vertigo
and prickling palms, ambassadors infected
with the shore from whence the creatures came.
In all victories like this one, the island gains

so much and that is less of everything.
Homes slacken and crack, horses
travel the unlit roads, termites mate
like buzzing thorns in wall and tree,
and somewhere there is a whisper of
a legend, a stampede of cows flying
and galloping straight to stomachs;
the marabú rising and grinding to charcoal,
hard and hacking and constant,
among flowers that grow from absolutely nothing,
which the crocodiles eat as well, dark hearted
and tide-cursed and hurting too
and crying at the bay, writhing to be let in.

You are another maimed force
expelled from sun and water,
and Cuba wins more sanctions,
more hunger, more, more, more,
there can always be more privation,
more Cuban loss, more Cuban debt,
more Cuban illness, perpetually sickened,
plague on the table, on the snout, in the city,
in the wormy reptiles, and who could
ever want the country to change?
This place could never end.

Trump Meeting Kim Jong-Un

"I need a hero's welcome," the President said,
a bite of Pyongyang instead of Singaporean
summits, a ferocity of when *he* was there,
Che Guevara, friendly champion, jail keeper,
and shirt. Car rides and hand waving, screaming
fans of that gleaming seaside purpose, a glory
not yet permitted to what all rulers would want.

For if the army fatigues could have become
scale armor, a silver bird speaking Spanish
over Che's head and the beret you can buy
as a souvenir in Havana turned to crown,

then it was possible that each magpie
dropped a feather in tribute,
the clouds welcoming the butcher
as sky king, winter's rainbow to fracture
on his skull. So he gained the power
of teleportation, and called North Korea
a template for what Cuba should be.
The template took hold. The
two countries teleported
into each other.

I heard that whenever on a shirt or a
mural, the eyes are real—they see.
Hats are huge things. Che sees you.
Trump watches you. The yearning
for teleportation, invisibility, tokens
of the divine luck. Every little boy and
each little girl's best friend with
Special Leader powers: toddlers
crammed at the border, a parade
for stomping soldiers, or to think
to overthrow Maduro in Venezuela,
the remains of little empire dreams.

Americans found Fidel fascinating
because he went to New York, rode
a carousel, and pounded his teeth
over a hot dog.

The UN was changed forever.
After Fidel dies, for three days and
nights North Korea mourns,
Kim Jong-Un bowing in memory to
a framed photo in the embassy,
fellow invincible friend, magic master,
thinking the Spanish words he
knows, until he, too, disappears.

Abuelas

Democracy does not flower,
as if the communism of my
grandfather passes from him
to me to the roots underneath
Miami. The castles are too high,
the yachts too fast on the sea.

Though Castro is now dead,
Lillian does not return either,
last living grandmother.
Inwardly, some heart and
memory swells and paces
until the Alzheimer's takes
her too, until she claims
that Fidel is at the door
por una visita, broken mind
allowing her to bid us
to open the door and simply
let the blooded ghost in.

VICTORIA MARÍA CASTELLS
is a creative writing teacher in Miami, Florida.
Her poems have appeared in *Reservoir*,
The Journal, *Quarter After Eight*, *Notre Dame Review*,
and other literary journals.

Printed in the USA
CPSIA information can be obtained
at www.ICGtesting.com
LVHW011811240823
756138LV00004B/367